Miley Cyrus

Katie Franks

PowerKiDS press.

New York

Published in 2009 by The Rosen Publishing Group, Inc.
29 East 21st Street, New York, NY 10010

First Edition

Editor: Nicole Pristash
Book Design: Kate Laczynski
Photo Researcher: Jessica Gerweck

Photo Credits: Cover, p. 1, 8, 11, 16, 20 © Getty Images, Inc; p. 4 © Jeff Kravitz/Getty Images; p. 7 © Ron Galella, Ltd./Getty Images; p. 12 © Jesse Grant/Getty Images; p. 15 © Bennett Raglin/Getty Images; p. 19 © AP Images.

Library of Congress Cataloging-in-Publication Data

Franks, Katie.
  Miley Cyrus / Katie Franks.
       p. cm. — (Kid stars!)
  Includes index.
  ISBN 978-1-4042-4467-2 (library binding) ISBN 978-1-4042-4532-7 (pbk)
  ISBN 978-1-4042-4550-1 (6-pack)
  1. Cyrus, Miley, 1992– —Juvenile literature. 2. Singers—United States—Biography—Juvenile literature.
3. Actresses—United States—Biography—Juvenile literature. I. Title.
  ML3930.C98F73 2009
  782.42164092—dc22
  [B]
                                         2007052763

Manufactured in the United States of America

Contents

Meet Miley Cyrus.................................5

It Runs in the Family 6

Getting into Acting 9

Auditioning for Disney 10

Hannah Montana 13

Life as a Pop Star 14

The Best of Both Worlds Tour 17

Everything Hannah! 18

What's Next?..................................21

Fun Facts 22

Glossary 23

Index 24

Web Sites 24

Miley Cyrus has many fans around the world. Young girls look up to Miley and her character Hannah Montana because they both set a good example for girls.

Meet Miley Cyrus

Miley Cyrus became an overnight **sensation** as the star of the Disney Channel's *Hannah Montana*. In less than a year, Miley was not only the star of a hit TV show, but she was also singing at sold-out **concerts** all over the United States.

Although her fame came quickly, Miley has a strong family standing behind her, and it helps keep her feet on the ground. With her talent and her family's help, Miley hopes to stay a successful star. Let's take a look at Miley's life, *Hannah Montana*, and what Miley hopes to do in the coming years!

It Runs in the Family

Destiny Hope Cyrus was born on November 23, 1992, in Franklin, Tennessee. Her dad used to call her Smiley when she was little, and that name turned to Miley. On January 29, 2008, Miley changed her name to Miley Ray Cyrus.

Miley's father is Billy Ray Cyrus. He is a country singer and an actor. Miley's mother is named Leticia. Miley also has five brothers and sisters. Her family is very close, and going to church is one of their **favorite** things to do together. Miley says she is lucky to have such a big, strong family to count on.

Here Miley is seen with her father, Billy Ray Cyrus, in Tennessee. Miley was around two years old when this picture was taken.

When Miley was looking for acting jobs, she stayed positive. Her father told her not to get too sad if she did not get a part she wanted.

Getting into Acting

Miley wanted to be an actress from a young age. As a kid, she would make her family watch her sing and dance.

When Miley was nine years old, the Cyrus family moved to Toronto, Canada. There, she got her first acting role, or part. It was on the TV show *Doc*, which starred Miley's dad. That same year, Miley got her first movie role, in *Big Fish*. She played a little girl named Ruthie. After the movie ended, Miley looked for more acting jobs because she loved acting so much.

Auditioning for Disney

Miley sent a **video** of herself to Disney when she was 11. The video was an **audition** for a role on a Disney TV show. The people at Disney liked Miley, but they thought she was too young. It was only after they had looked at 1,000 more kids that they called Miley back to audition again.

Miley did very well on her second audition. She did so well as an actress and a singer that she was picked to be the star of her own show. She was going to play Hannah Montana!

Miley not only sings, but she also plays the piano and the guitar. Miley has also written more than 100 songs!

Here Miley (center) is seen with some of the cast of *Hannah Montana*. Miley's father, Billy Ray (second from left), even plays her father on the show!

Hannah Montana

On *Hannah Montana*, Miley Cyrus plays Miley Stewart. Miley Stewart is a teen girl, who just moved to California from Tennessee. She has to deal with school, friends, and all the problems that teens face. However, Miley Stewart has a secret. She is also a pop star, named Hannah Montana. Only her two best friends, her brother, and her father know. On the show, Miley tries to live her everyday life and be a famous singer at the same time.

Hannah Montana was a big hit from its very first **episode**. Around three **million** people tune in to follow Hannah's **adventures** each week!

Life as a Pop Star

While playing Hannah Montana, Miley got to sing and see what it would be like to be a pop star. Not long after the show began, Miley put out an album as her character Hannah. More than two million albums were sold!

Soon, Miley began to write her own songs. She wanted to put out her own album, too. In the summer of 2007, when she was 15, Miley made the album *Hannah Montana 2: Meet Miley Cyrus*. It has two disks. On one disk, Miley sings as Hannah, on the other, she sings as herself.

Being a pop star means spending time with your fans.
Here Miley is signing some posters for her fans in New York City.

Miley says that nothing else matters when she steps out on stage. Miley does not think of singing as work because she has so much fun doing it!

The Best of Both Worlds Tour

By 2007, Miley had a hit show and two best-selling albums. She had even sung as Hannah Montana live, when she opened for The Cheetah Girls on their 2006 concert **tour**. Miley had done so well with The Cheetah Girls that Disney made a tour just for Miley that year.

For this tour, Miley sang both as Hannah Montana and as herself. She sang songs from her album *Hannah Montana 2: Meet Miley Cyrus*. The tour was called the Best of Both Worlds Tour. Tickets for these concerts sold out in minutes, which made Hannah Montana and Miley Cyrus even more famous.

Everything Hannah!

When Disney noticed how **popular** *Hannah Montana* was, it began to work with Miley to make lots of different goods that have to do with the show. In 2007, a store called Macy's began selling a *Hannah Montana* clothing line. The clothes are just like the ones Hannah wears on her show. There are also *Hannah Montana* toys and a fun web site.

All this extra work does not tire Miley out, though. Even though it can sometimes get in the way of her schoolwork, she enjoys it. She says Disney has let her do everything she loves.

In this picture, Miley shows off her *Hannah Montana* clothing line in New York City.

Miley loves to perform, whether that be singing or acting, because it makes people happy. She says she has the best job in the world!

What's Next?

Miley Cyrus is a very busy girl. To keep the family close, the Cyrus family moved to Los Angeles, where *Hannah Montana* is made. The Cyrus kids were sad to leave behind old friends and the family's seven horses. However, sticking together as a family was more important·and they have helped each other deal with the move.

What's next for Miley? Miley loves to **perform**. Singing and acting for a living have been her dream since she was a little girl. Miley will keep performing for a long time. She wants to **entertain** people for years to come!

MILEY CYRUS

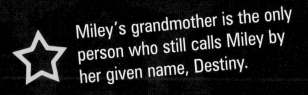 Miley's grandmother is the only person who still calls Miley by her given name, Destiny.

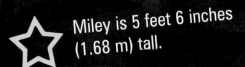 Miley is 5 feet 6 inches (1.68 m) tall.

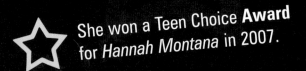 She won a Teen Choice **Award** for *Hannah Montana* in 2007.

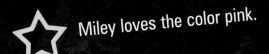 Miley loves the color pink.

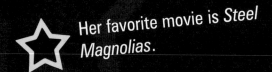 Her favorite movie is *Steel Magnolias*.

 Miley's favorite type of food is Chinese.

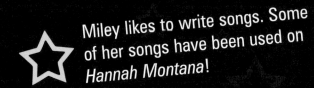 Miley likes to write songs. Some of her songs have been used on *Hannah Montana*!

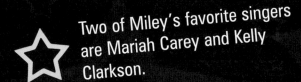 Two of Miley's favorite singers are Mariah Carey and Kelly Clarkson.

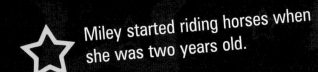 Miley started riding horses when she was two years old.

 Miley's favorite sport is cheerleading.

Glossary

adventures (ed-VEN-cherz) Different or fun things to do.

audition (ah-DIH-shun) A measure of the skills of an actor.

award (uh-WORD) A special honor given to someone.

concerts (KONT-serts) Public performances with music.

entertain (en-ter-TAYN) To keep someone interested or pleased.

episode (EH-puh-sohd) One show of a TV show's run.

favorite (FAY-vuh-rut) Most liked.

million (MIL-yun) A very large number.

perform (per-FORM) To sing, dance, or act in front of other people.

popular (PAH-pyuh-lur) Liked by lots of people.

sensation (sen-SAY-shun) Something that is very good.

tour (TUHR) When a singer or band travels to different places
   to perform.

video (VIH-dee-oh) A taped performance of something.

Index

B
Best of Both Worlds
    Tour, 17
Big Fish, 9

C
Cheetah Girls, The,
    17
concerts, 5, 17
Cyrus, Billy Ray
    (father), 6

Cyrus, Leticia
    (mother), 6

D
Disney, 5, 10, 17, 18
Doc, 9

H
Hannah Montana, 5,
    13

*Hannah Montana 2:
    Meet Miley Cyrus*,
    14, 17

L
Los Angeles,
    California, 21

T
Toronto, Canada, 9

Web Sites

Due to the changing nature of Internet links, PowerKids Press has developed an online list of Web sites related to the subject of this book. This site is updated regularly. Please use this link to access the list:
www.powerkidslinks.com/kids/miley/